Our Wonderful World

By the Pupils of
MARYHILL PRIMARY SCHOOL

PRINTED & PUBLISHED BY:
WINE PRESS, 1 SILVER STREET, TAMWORTH
01827 67622

Maryhill Primary School
March 1997
ISBN 1 86237 000 1 £4.00

In this book we have tried to capture the different aspects of our wonderful world. We hope you enjoy reading it as much as we enjoyed writing it.

Gemma

World of Play and Sport

Nature's everywhere

Nature nature everywhere
nature nature in the air
Birds snug up inside the tree
Asleep as the day cools down and the light becomes week
The morning becomes fresh and the light has his strength
for another nice day in the country

By Phillip Maxwell

I Love Animals

I love birds
I watch them fly and play,
They like to eat worms and bread
When they fly they glide and sway.

Spiders are black and hairy
They scurry around all day,
I think there're horrible and scary
With thier big long legs.

People think that rats are smelly
Because they live in the sewers,
Some rats live in peoples welly
And get troden on and bite.

My favourite animal I must say
Is a hampster also cute,
But sometimes they escape
And crawl into my boot.

By
Jessica Barnes
age 10

The Match
England v Italy

Today England are playing Italy at Wembely. England have a good chance of winning. Alan Shearer and Teddy Sheringham have kickoff Sheringham passes to Gascoigne Gascoigne to Neville a big kick by Neville finds Shearer Shearer shoots and Scores England take the lead by a goal it back to the start for Italy Del piro to kickoff Di matteo with a slow shoot by Matteo Its dipping! Its gone in! Italy have Equalized! Seaman never had a chance..... and theres the final whistle. Italy 1 england 1

by

Andrew Lownds

The european championships.   The opening ceremony of the championships was an exciting event. There were countries from all over Europe. England were going to prove a point to the other teams.

They played Spain in the quarter finals. It was a very tight match which went to penalties. David Seaman took England to the semi finals against Germany.

Andrew Poole, Lee Oliver and Mark Capewell will report from Wembeley "England to kick off shearer to ince plays a long ball to macmanaman to neville crosses it to shearer its a GOAL one nil to england.

Germany take the kick off rossler to muller takes one takes two shoots great save by seaman! southgate clears it gascoine takes muller gets fouled its a penalty ince takes it its a goal two nil to england rossler muller shoots scores. England lose it rossler goal england have lost it england lose it again three nil and the whistle blows Germany have won three two.
Lee Oliver

Our wonderful world of Sports and Games.

I like football.
Football is exciting to play. If the ball goes out it is a throw in to the team mate. In football you need team work. If you commit a foul in football you get a yellow or red card.
If you get a yellow card it's just a normal foul however if you get a red card, your out of the game. Football takes skill and fitness. Football players work as a team.

By Clare Golden
Age 8.

I want to be a great footballer I am brilliant at sports I will play for Stoke and England Tomas

The Match.

It's going to be a very, very exiting match today with Manchester United vs Wimbledon. If Man.Utd win they will win the Carling premership. Liverpool are playing Newcastle. If Liverpool win their match they'll win the premership. Now here are your Commentators Andy Gray & Martain Tyler. They've kicked off now. Oliver to Capewell look at them go, oh yes it's a goal!!! Man Utd have scored after 90 seconds!. (Half time possted) Wimbledon to Kickoff Earle is tackled by Capewell he takes one, two, three! Capewell has scored in the 88th minute PEEP, PEEP, PEEP. There's the final whistle! Man.Utd have 2-0 and Liverpool have lost 7-1. Their going crazy down their. Walking up for the Cup. Capewell has done it scoring both goal. by Mark Capewell.

Football

football is so great
I play it every day
I score a lot of goals
Its easy to play
and it keeps you healthy

My favourite team is Liverpool
I really think they are cool
Mc Manaman is the best player
He scores lots of goals
thats why he's my favourite
player.

Josh Eyres

I wpht to be a fqst
runner and wlr a trophy
on sports Doy

S hphe

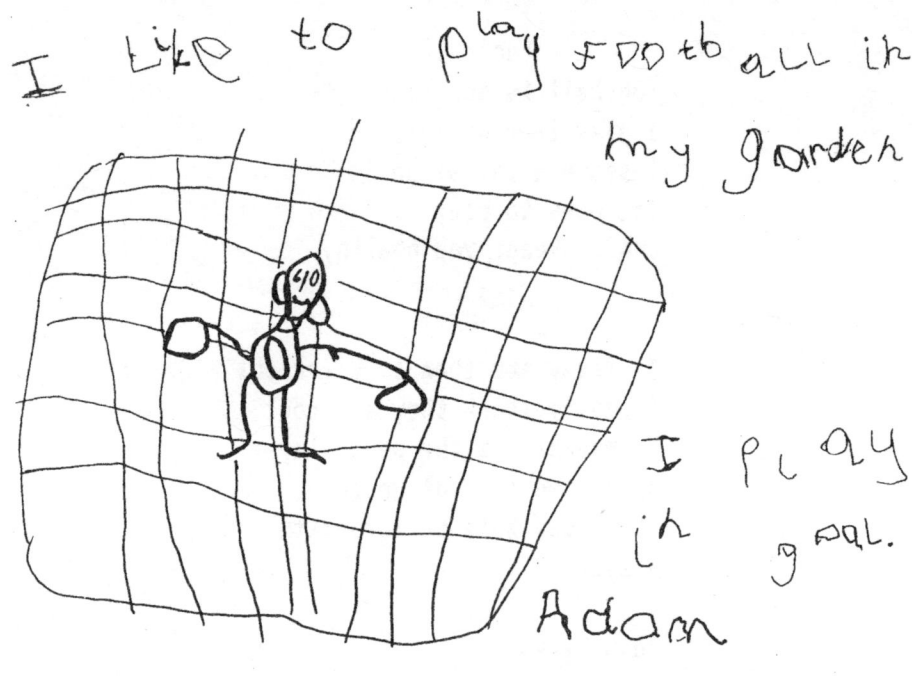

Sport

Tennis is great fun
Netball makes you sweat,
Gymnastics is athletic
It makes your forehead wet.

Football mostly is for boys
Cricket is for spring,
Rounders is my favourite sport
You run round in a ring.

Volley balls completely ace
In snooker you pot balls,
Swimming is quite O.K
Rowing drives you up the walls.
        By Amy
            Jones.

I am playing football for stoke

Michael.

Our wonderful world of sports

My favourite sport is basketball because you can hold the ball and jog with it. It is better than netball because you can do any throw in the net. The thing I don't like about basketball is that you can't run with the ball. I also like football. It is brilliant being in goals. You can hold the ball in the box. I also like hockey, I like takling.

by Martin fallows

Our Wonderfl World of Soccer

When I go to a football match I am excited and I want some one to score a goal. I like to shout I don't like yellow cards or red cards because the teams should play fair. I enjoy Football It's fun and wondeuful

by Kyle Watson   age 8

I am training to be a footballer. I will play for England.

Karl

I wont to be an athlete and win lots of medals.

kyle

Sports

On sports Day I sometimes win and sometimes lose. If I get first I get a red card. You are second if you get a yellow card

By Joanne Oxley

I like sport. My favourite sport is football. I like horse riding. I play football and I win horse riding medals. I've got 4 medals and a football trophey

by Timothy Lee Horsfield

I like playing with my sister and with my sandpit and I like playing with my garaage it is dead big I can put 20 cars in it and I love it I played with it. And I like playing house.

Stephen Age 6

Football is so great
I play it every day
I score lots of goals
Its easy to play

My favourite team is Liverpool
I really think they're cool
I watch them when i can
My favourite players Mcmanaman

I Play for my school
on the wing is where I play
we win most of our matches
At home and away!   By Joshua
                        Eyres

If you are getting ready for sports Day at home you can practise the egg and spoon race with a potato and spoon and keep running up and down. I like being in the egg and spoon race.

Rich, West

I Like to play Football. I play with my brother in my garden. I scored 10 goal Lloyd scored 19 goal

Lucas 1

Sport Day

On sports day I was in the running Race and I came fifth I won Steven and I came Last and then the sports were over.

by David Harry

I like to go to Blackpool and I did and I went on The Big wheel and I had a ice cream Then I went on the bumper Then I went on the coach and I had a bust

Matthew

Sports

I like Football Because you can Score goals and you can have Penalties and I like running But some times I lose.

By David Lear
8 Years

Play

I Like to Play house because it is Nice. Your friends can Play. and I Like doing The Splits. and Your brother can do The Splits.

Kayleigh

I like playing football in my back gardeng with my brothe and my siste with a leather foot ball

Dean

I like sporps beacuse they do the races it is good games beacuse a game i like a game is to play with.

Ashley G 6

I like to dance beoause I think it is funny. I like to twiis around and around. I like to do the splits. and then I put the whole dance together

Rachel Hosey Age 6

I Like to go to play at my Frends house. I Like to play at Football as Wall. And I like play on my game. And I like to have a birthday too. And I like to play with Daniel And it is good Fun

Philip 7

I like to play on my bike.
Because I can go fast.
And I like to play Football.
Because Ic.
IS good

Rachael
6

Sport

I Like to Dance because it is Fun and I Like to Twiss around Thats why I Like it is good Dance is very excting Dance with other People

april ashton 6

I Like Playing With my friend. We Play house And School. We Went out side. it was good then we went Back in. then We made a cake. We had Some it was nice. then We Went home And we had Some tea. then we went to Bed. Danielle Taylor 7

I like to play football in the park with my Dad. I can win him. Football is good fun

Daniel
class 4

I like playing football because I like running. I like running the ball.

Beth 7

I like netball because you have to throw the ball in the sky. And try to get the ball in the net. And catch it so you can have another go before some body gets it.

Nicole Leese 7cl4

Sport

my favourite sport is football because I like when stoke city score my best bit of football is when people score goals. football is a hard game to play

Jake Hyise

World of Pets

The Pet Shop

One day I was walking passed A pet shop and I saw a nice dog. I said How Much is that dog in The window the one with the waggly tail and he said it is £20 I bouht the nice dog I took it home and gave it some food I took it for lots of walks in the fields

Steven ι
age 11

A rabbit has sharp teeth and if you put your hand By wayne Carroll age 9. by its mouth it might bite you. Rabbit eat carrots and Rabbit food. We let him run about and keep him warm in a cage. In the summer you can let him out to run around. I love my rabbit and he makes my world wonderful.

our wonderful world

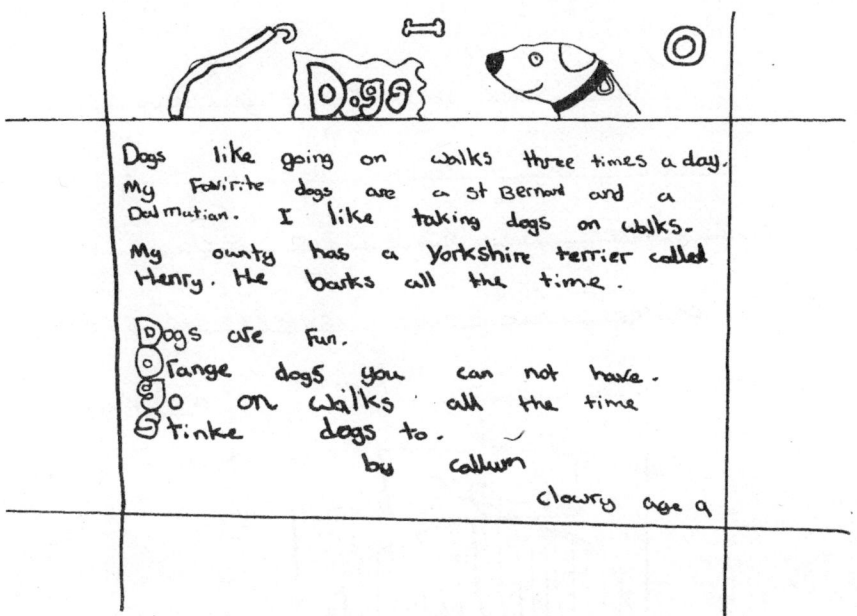

Dogs like going on walks three times a day.
My Favirite dogs are a St Bernard and a
Dalmatian. I like taking dogs on walks.
My ounty has a Yorkshire terrier called
Henry. He barks all the time.

Dogs are Fun.
Orange dogs you can not have.
Go on walks all the time
Stinke dogs to.
　　　by callum
　　　　　clowry age 9

Peet's Pets Poem

Theres a cat with a rat on the front of the matt.
Theres a ox with a fox on top of the rocks
Theres a dragon with Adam. and there sleeping with madm
Theres a Bour with mrs moore by the back door
Theres a Tiger with some cider and he sleeping with a miner
Theres a monkey that is funkey and he thinks he his hunky
Theres a Ram with a poem and he Ron over the man
Theres a Moase with a goose and hes drinking the Juice.

Daniel Peet
age 10

GARY Imber

Age 10

I LOVE PETS

I like pets because they are very cute my favites pet is a Labrador is nane is Zeka He loves me to Bits He sleeps In a Basket in my Bed room.

Dogs

I like cats because they sleep on me. they purr when you stroke them.

by Samantha Garside

The pet poem

One day there was a dog his name was ben bod.
one day there was a cat that ate a fat rat.
once there was a bat that ate some fat.

sarah Golden
Age 9

I would like a hamster for a pet.
by Jessica winter

My Fish

My fish is called Faye. She doesn't know how to play. She goes around the tank all day. And has a friend called clay.

By Scott McCartney age 10

Parrots are green are hard to be seen.

A snake swims in the lake and is thin as a rake.

A deer likes to drink beer in the summer sun.

by Gemma Adams
Age 10

I-like-my-pet rabbit

I-play-with-it.

-by-stephanie-sallis

My cat is called Misty.
She is black and white.

By Dominee Colclough.

I wish I had a hamster
I'd call it Gary and
give it food and water.
by Ganymi Chalak

All about Pets

I have 1 hamster and 1 guinea pig and 1 dog. The puppies were sold. Melissa had 1 Katie had 1 and Sharon had 1 and when the puppies left Sophie was crying and we miss them

By

Emma Jayne Roberts

I love my hamster because I feed him.

by Matthew Glover

I am having a guinea pig and my sister is having a rabbit

by Nicholas Harris

I want my cat to stay in the house so he won't fight.

By Lewis Franklin.

I have got a kitten he likes to play.

by Roseanne Johnson

pets

I have got 2 rabbits. They are called poppy and Sally. I give them rabbit food and sometimes biscuits. Sometimes I pick them up and cuddle them. When it is sunny I let them run in the garden.

By Samantha Surtees I

My pet is a dog.
He has a black ear and a white body.
His name is Buster.
I had a cat but he died.

By Stefan Williams.

Pets

I have got 5 pets one is a dog called Axle. He is a and when we say walkies he goes mad. we have got 1 hamster once we lost him. I found him under my bed. I have got tow birds. Their names are Sparky and missy. we have also got 1 fish.

by Rylan

I like my rabbit because he jumps

by Kevin Booth

I have 1 cat. 🐱
His name is mr. Bill Bow
Bagins. He has stripes on his
back and he's got green eyes.
He likes to play with birds
and rips their heads off.
Sometimes he brings back
plastic bags for presents. He
hardly comes in Because he likes it out
side. Once he came up stairs and
slept with me. He is a boy.   by Nicole G
                              Age 7

My Pets

My name is Emma. I have one
hamster and 5 rabbits. I like
hamsters because they keep
me company and they tickle

me on my hands and I like
giving them food.

BY emma cartlidge

PETS

My pets are Tammy Tabby and Dusty. Tammy normally chases the cats they do not like it. Dusty brings sweet wrappers to the window sill she sits there until we let her in.

by Craig Whitehead

pets.

My cat is named Tiger because he has stripes like a Tiger. Tiger goes hunting like a Tiger. Tiger can open a door because he is clever. Tiger is clever because I train him. He catches rats and bites their heads off.

Daniel Hughes

My pets

I have got 2 pets a rabbit and a guineapig. Their names are Sooty and Sweep. Sweep is fluffy and Sooty is sweet. I Love them both all the same. I get them out every day. Sweep likes cuddles Sooty likes cuddles too.

By Rhian Taylor

I Love my Dog very much. Me and Dad take her in the car every Day. My Dog comes in my room at 6:30 every day. I play with her. I give my Dog food. I give her a bath every week every week I give her a bone

from Mark Hamnett

My Pets.

One day I went to feed my gerbils and the mother gerbil had a baby and I taught her to lie and sit. In the night my gerbils died and in the morning me and my mum went to get me 2 rabbits and my mum said I could have another if my rabbits died.

By Kirsty Boote

Pets

Hi my name is Sophie and I have got a hamster and I think he I's funny because he hangs on the bars of his cage and I think he is funny because he fell off his house when he was asleep and my mum thought he was dead but then he woke up.

By Sophie Lownds

Pets

I have a rabbit and some fish and my fish just swim around and my Rabbit plays with me and when ever I feed her she goes straight to the food and when I close the hutch door she scratches the door and her name is Daisy. I like Hamsters and gerbils because they tickle my hands and I like them and they like me. by Melissa Acston Age 7 years

pets.

I have got a pet cat called Tiggy who's very clever. She can open the door, jump off the roof knock on windows and climb in the beds. She is spotty she is clever

by David Gallimore

I have got 5 pets
One dog 2 cats and
2 birds. I love all
my pets. When I take my
dog for a walk in the snow
She bounces in it and once
my cats slipped on the ice.
All of pets are different ages.
Tess my dog loves the snow. But
my cats don't.

Alexandra Paczezowski
age 8

The special dog

Once there was a girl called Zoe who was six and she said every christmas and every birthday,"Please mum can I have a dog?" and all the time her mum said "no!"

Zoe was an only child so she had no one to play with when her friends went out. That's why she wanted a dog.

The next day was Zoe's birthday and she was not excited at all! She went downstairs. There were loads of presents but no dog. Then she heard a dog barking. She ran into the kitchen and there was a big dalmation. Zoe said,"This is the best birthday ever! I will call her Spot.

Zoe took Spot for a walk every day and loved him very much.

Danielle Adams

World of Hobbies

my hobbies

my favourite hobby is
singing and dancing because
I *♪♪♪* want to be a pop star
I always said to myself
be a pop star. So that is what
I want to be.

Samantha Maggie
7 year Redfer old

Shaun Bould

I go karate and I got my BLACK belt

and made a friend

and I play went my friends and we have good fun.

Hobbies

My Hobby is drawing
I like drawing it is fun.
I draw cars.
I like cars.

Ben Briggs

Hobbies.

My hobby is keyrings. Some have water in them and some sing. My first keyring was Bart Simpson.

by Danny McGarry

My hobbies

My favourite hobbies are football and computers. I want to grow up to be a lorry driver and that is all I wont to be.

by Jamie Lewis 8 years

I go to karate lessons and I have a BLUE Belt and I saw my mate at the karate lessons and he had a GOLD Belt

Hobbies

I go gymnasties with mr Anney and I do vault and pairs routine and morning gym

Daniel Greatbatch.

My name is Lucy. My favourite hobby is karate. I am a red belt. My best kata is Kion. My favourite teacher is george. He is a black belt. I go with daniel Haywood and my brother. My favourite kick is myagery. My friend is Nat. I go because I like it and because when go out to a disco you can look after your self. So I'll see you soon.

By Lucy Ellen Hodgkinson

Hobbies.

Hello my name is Abigail and I am here to tell you about my hobbies. Number one going Avoning with my mum. Number two tidying my room which is boring. Number 3 Watching children's BBC and Itv. Number 4 ringing people on the Phone.

By Abigail Jade Brigham.

My hobby

My hobby is horse riding because I like horses and ponies because they are very fast. I know how to brain a horse and a pony and a donkey

By Samantha Meadowcroft

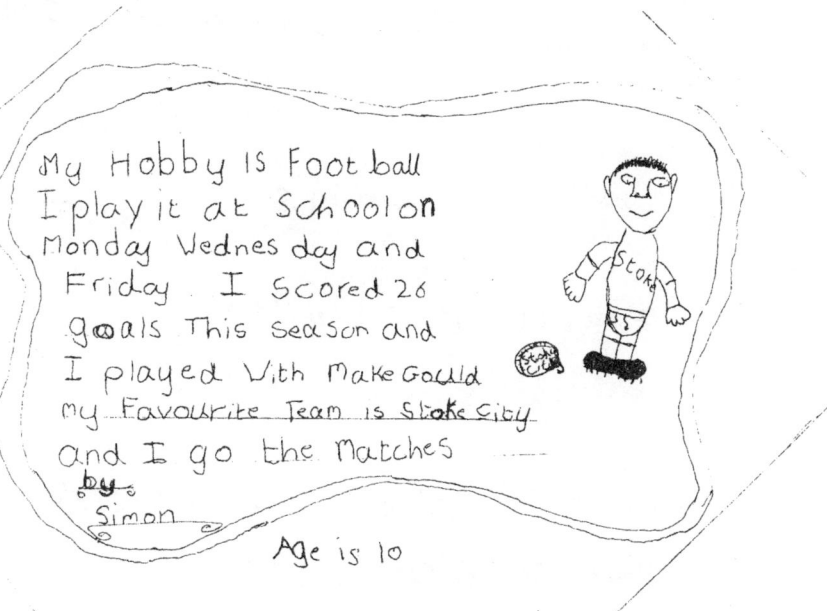

My Hobby is Football I play it at school on Monday Wednesday and Friday. I Scored 26 goals This season and I played with Make Gould my Favourite Team is Stoke City and I go the matches
by
Simon

Age is 10

Myself

Hello my name is Cara Clowry. I go to Maryhill Primary School. I have a brother Callum. He also goes to Maryhill Primary School. My hobbies are gymnastics, horse riding, Skating and swimming. My favourite hobby is gymnastics I go every night except for Thursdays. Susan and I are doing pairs work we do our routine to Electric Salsa.   By Cara Clowry

Aged 11

I wish I could sleep at my cousins house.
by Daniel Darlington

I like to go on my tractor.
I like to play on it.

By Daniel Goodwin

I wish mrs Hughes had hard work.
by Adam Farrall

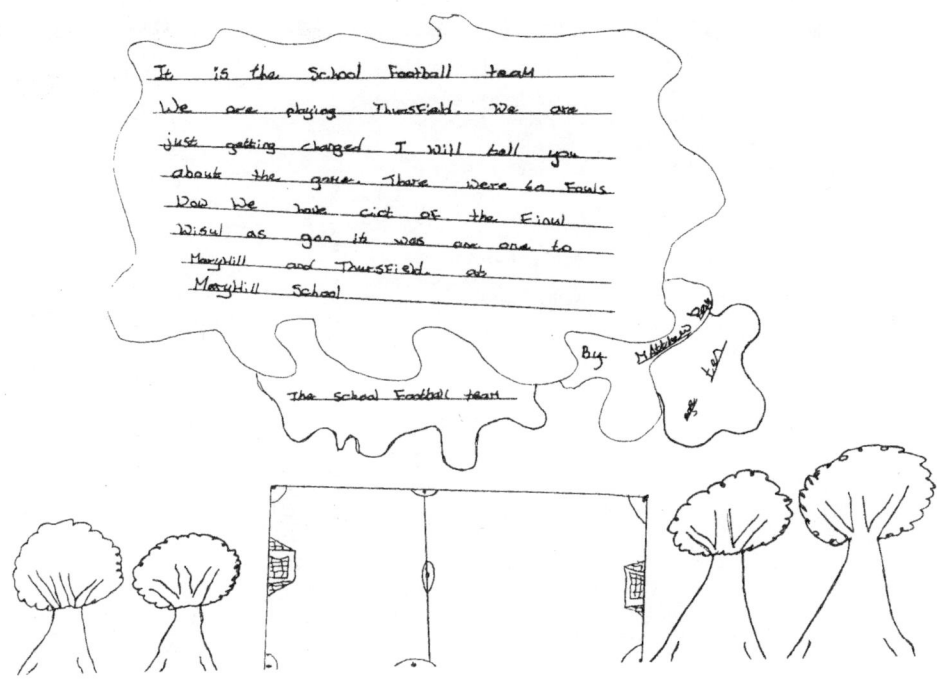

My name is Donna Smith my favourite hobby is netball. I like playing netball every day. I like making my bedroom a mess and I like being silly like a clown. I like throwing my teddies. I like playing on my bike and going to Bathpool to feed the ducks and then to the park.
  By Donna Smith.

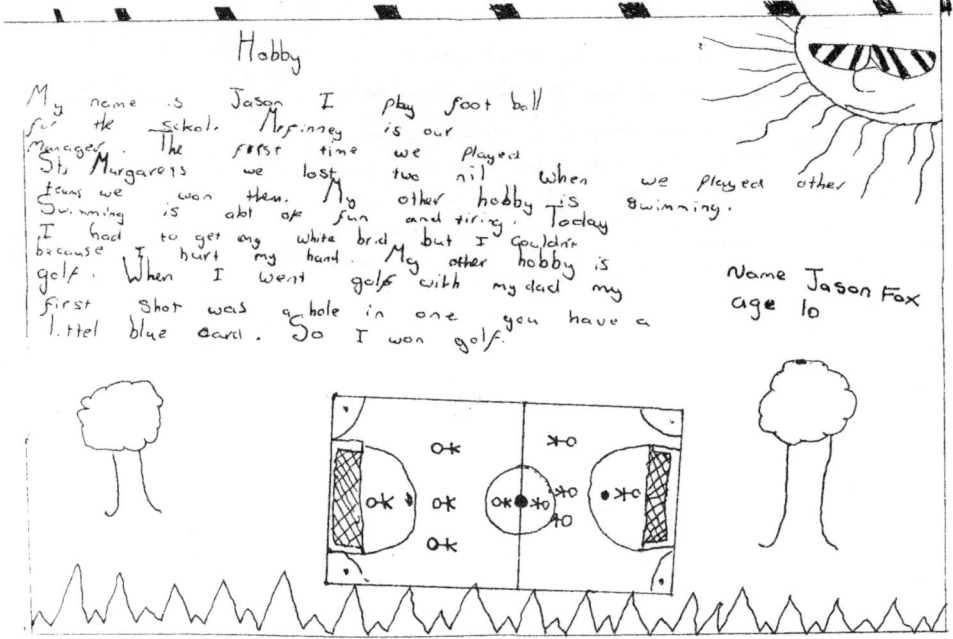

Hobby

My name is Jason I play football for the school. Mr Finney is our manager. The first time we played St Margarets we lost two nil. When we played other teams we won them. My other hobby is swimming. Swimming is a lot of fun and tiring. Today I had to get my white brid but I couldn't because I hurt my hand. My other hobby is golf. When I went golf with my dad my first shot was a hole in one you have a littel blue card. So I won golf.

Name Jason Fox
age 10

Hobbies By Lesley Downing

I have 3 hobbies that I Like best. The Best hobby is swimming. another one is collecting things. The thing I Like collecting is Figures and toys. I have got 100 and some thing. I also Like riding my bike up hills

My hobby is running. I am fast at running and skipping and football and rugby I am very good at fishing and baking.

by christopher Brown

My hobby is playing on my computer I like to play a game called Grand Prix. This is a game for one player. The person playing the game as to pick a track. The next thing that you do is to choose a position where you want to start. Afterwards you start the game by pressing the letter A. That makes the car that is on the track to accelerate. Then you can start the race. If you want to have a look outside of the car you can press the left arrow key. If you want to get out of the game is to press the escape and it will take you to the main menu and clik on Eixt to dos. I like go on window to play on Easykey and play music is fun on a cd-rom.

Daniels Hobby

Age 10

My Hobby

My hobby is horse riding and one day when it was raining I fell off my horse and my Nanny laughed at me and thats all I can say Natalie L Poulson

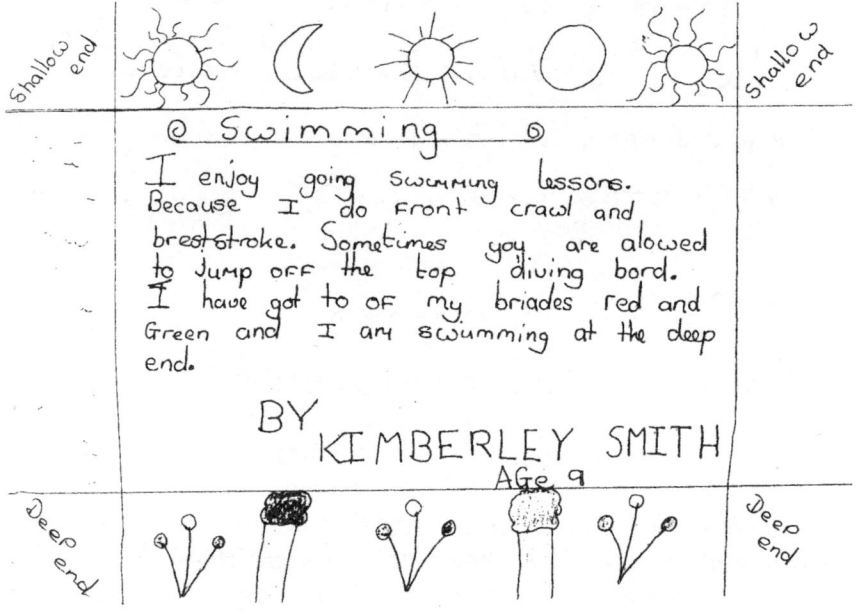

Swimming

I enjoy going swimming lessons. Because I do front crawl and breststroke. Sometimes you are alowed to jump off the top diving bord. I have got to of my briades red and Green and I am swimming at the deep end.

BY KIMBERLEY SMITH
Age 9

Hobbies.

I like walking because it's exciting and you can get big muscles and I can walk to my friend house.
Cleaning is one of my favourite hobbies because I can clean up all the kitchen and I can clean up the oven too.
I also like baking, because you can get food all over your hands and it is sloppy.
Learning is a good hobby too, because you can learn about alot of things.
I also like climbing aswell because I can climb very high and I can make a tree swing and a tree house.
I like reading too, because it's good because when you read you learn too.

by Katie Sanderson
class 8, age 9.

Swimming

Swimming is a sport that lots of people enjoy. There are many different swimming strokes, breast stroke, front crawl, back stroke and butterfly. Swimming is fun and you can get lots of badges. I have my white braid which means I can swim very well.

Swimming is fun
We go swimming on monday
I told this poem because
Me and
My friends
Infants too
Now what to do
Going swimming today too

By Matthew Gough age 8

▪ Reading ▪

Reading is fun.

Every body knows.

And it is very interesting.

Dad is reading all the time.

I get books with my money.

Noels House party book is good.

Glad my reading poem is ending.

by Christopher Wilkinson age 8

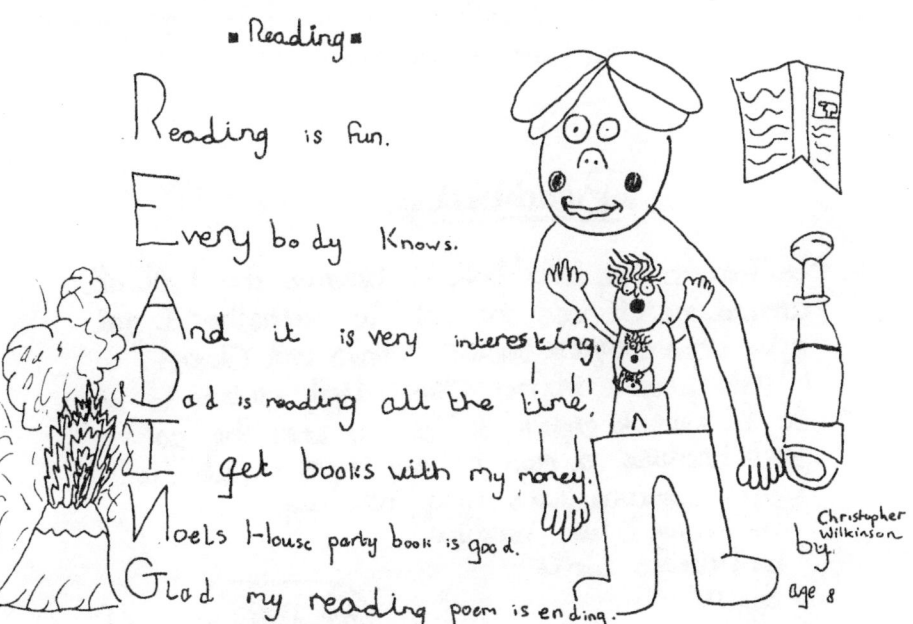

Our wonderful world of hobbies.

I have two hobbies they are piano playing and swimming. Piano playing is hard to srart but once you get started it gets easier. I am on grade one. Swimming is quite hard to learn it is hard to skull and quite hard to tread water. Football is easy to play but hard to learn skills. Rugby is hard it's a very fast game and very good.

By Daniel Finn

Karate

At Karate when you have to be careful that you don't pull a muscle and when you punch aswell. There are all sorts of kicks punches and blocks I like the knife hand block and punch and I like the side kick and the turning kick.

By Nathan Ellerton

Benchball

When I play benchball I bounce the ball all around me. We toss the ball to eachother. I feel active when everyone shouts, cheers and claps! Most people in my class don't no how to play so I have to explain it. You no when the game starts because a man or lady blows a whistle. When someone wins they all hug. That's why I like benchball!
by Rebecca Turner
age 9

World of Nature

The Forest was going to be knocked down to make way for a new road. One day an ox and his friends went to a new forest called Green hill but they did not know it had wolves. The ox and his friends got attacked. Shouldn't we consider the animals and their homes.

Andrew Phillips
age 10

Worms wiggle

Worms wiggle
bugs juggle
rabbits hop
horse clop
Snake slide
Seagulls glide
mice creep
Horses leep
puppies talk
Kittens stalk

by Laura Wood
Age 9

Winter I like

Winter winter in the sky
the Dark cold nights I
wonder why.

Stiff white fingers
and rock stone legs
and fallen twigs whatames

Can not wait until
its Summer then go
to My Aunt and play
with my Brother.

by Adam
Maxwell
Age 11

I'm glad that I live near a park for in the Winter after dark I go out side and look around what wundaful world it is but some times it is not such a wundaful place to be I wish some times that all of the horrible things would go away the world would be a much bett place to be and we could be safe agane we should thank God for all the good things.

by Hayley Franklin
age 9

The Tree

Two men came along to cut the old tree.
They took the broken tree into the van.
It went to the facktory and made paper.
They put it in the van.
The van came to Mary Hill Primary School. Mrs Barker said thank you. She gave class 11 some paper to write this book.

Karen Haliwell
age 9

by Samantha Littleton
age 10

The Frosty night
I see a tree
Blowing and Blowing
I wonder why
I see Jack frost
Shivering and Shivering
under the tree
I wonder why?
I look at
the sky and
I wonder why
The stars shine bright
in the frosty night.

By Kimberley Potts
age 11

Dolphins

dolphins

I like dolphins because they play with me and splash me.
They make me excited and nice.
It looks fantastic when they tumble.
They sleep on the sea bed you know!
They make a squeaking noise.
I like it when they dive and when
They have a baby.
They bang their tail in the water.
by Alexandra Lillian Harris
age 9

Dolphins

I like dolphins because they are cute and they love to play with you. They splash and bang their tails in the water. They make a squeaking noise when they talk to each other. They sleep on the sea bed they also mate they swim quite slowly it depends what type of dolphin it is. I like baby dolphins best because they are very cute. And that is why I like dolphins.

by Tamzyn Jayne Brigham

age 8

I like rabbits because the rabbits are soft and I like animals that swim I like cat because they play with me and I like lions and I like flowers because you cha make chains

Alexa 6

I like nature because all the animals
My favourite animal is a cat. My cat goes to
sleep on my knee every day.

Stephen Blair

The flea

Henry the dog ran through a tree,
having fun until he felt a flea.
He had to run round the block,
because he had such a shock.
He itched,
He twitched,
he yelped,
he scratched.
He climbed a house where the roof was thatched.
He felt like such a goof,
because he fell through the roof.
Then he had a little cough
and the flea just fell off......
by Leigh Hughes

Don't kill us!

Bang Bang! "I've got one", said John, He had shot a gorilla. In the distance a lion was watching them and went and told friend tiger. They decided to kill John and his friend. Tiger and Lion hid behind a bush, and waited till they came into sight. They counted to 3 and pounced on the poachers and killed them! But Lion knew that they might have killed them poachers but their were still many poachers still shooting animals. Lion then noticed tiger was not there, so lion went to serch for him. He found him covered in blood. Then Lion said sadly "I wish they would all go away and leave us alone". And with that he lay down and cried.

By Ella Jane Burgess Age 11

I like Ladyirds because they crawl and like ladyirds because they are all red and blak and because they have Lots of legs

Jade 6

I like it when we go on the field and I can make daisy chains. Sometimes I find ladybirds. I like ladybirds because they have beautiful spots and bright colours. My favourite animal is a cat I wish I had a cat but my mummy will not let me.

Michelle Haworth 6

Wonderful world
polluting

Our world is a wonderful world because people do not fight. But this world will not stay wonderful if people keep polluting the air.

If people kept polluting the air it would start to kill the wild animals. And it would kill your cats or your dogs. So think before you pollute.

By Michael Rawlingson.

The Giraffe.

"Dad dad look there's a giraffe shoot quick" said Alex "Where?" said said Alex's dad Henry "It's over there in the trees LOOK!" said Alex "I can see it now" said Henry, There was a bang! and the giraffe fell to the ground. Alex and Henry ran over to it Alex said "This will make us a few bob wont it" Said Alex "Yes it will son" Said Henry. "Come on then dad how are we going to move it before the police get here" Said Alex "I've got a van in the lane" said Henry "I'll go and get it" "Hurry up and get it then or we will be in big trouble" said Alex.

They were loading the giraffe into the van when they heard police sirens. "We're going to be locked up" said Alex "Hurry up and we will make it" said Henry. So they jumped into the van and drove away. But the back of the van was not locked and the Giraffe fell out.

By Nicky Daly age 10.

I like butterflies.
They have nice colours.
They fly.
They used to be a caterpilllar.
They fly away if you go close.
And they are shy.

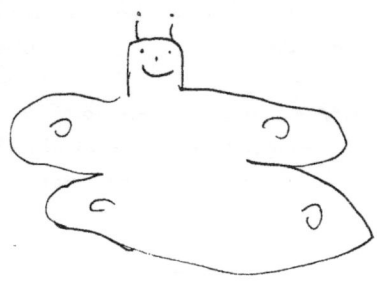

Adele 7

A tree has lots of creatures inside sometimes the bark is wobbly in the winter not all of the leaves fall off the trees. Naughty people climb the trees and the branches might break.

Ben E Age 6

Our wonderful world of Nature.

I think that it is very important that we do not pollute the sea and ponds. When an oil tanker got holed in an accident it spilled out tons and tons of oil into the sea. Thousands and thousands of seabirds and other sealife were killed. Seas, rivers, and streams are also polluted when factories leak unwanted chemicals into the waters of the world. It is not just pollution that is driving some animals to extinction it is also forests being cut down. Animals are losing their habitats and losing them fast. Animals like dormice. Dormice like sleeping at the bottoms of trees. The trees are disappearing quickly. I think that we should keep the world wonderful by not polluting seas and cutting down trees.

By: Katy Edgington.
Age 8.

Our Wonderful World Of nature   by Katie Mitchell

I like cats/Fish/rabbits/hedgehogs they are very soft and playful and loving. I enjoy feeding and nursing them. When Rosie my little kitten when she gets angry she bites my toes it tickles. I love cuddling my rabbits, they are very very soft and cute. My pets make my life wonderful.

Our wonderful world of nature

Nature is a wonderful thing.
You see rabbits running in fields.
Squirrels cimbing up the trees.
Dogs walking in the park
Robins getting worms from the
garden to feed their young.

by Laura heath age 9

by Laura Glover

Our wonderful world o Nature

I love my pet rabbit Floppy he is the best rabbit I have ever had. I sometimes forget about him and my mum or dad feed him. I love Floppy very very very much. I love cats the same because I have one his name is Fluff. My cats like playing with me because when I put my hand on his tummy it tickles him and he bites you and it hurts very much. I have 2 fish and we feed them and clean them out. The other animals I like are hedgehogs, they are cute. I like birds because I like them when they are babies because they are very cute. Animals make our wold wonderful.

Our wonderful world of Great white sharks.

The Great white shark is big and Strong. It can almost anything in the sea. Its teeth are sharp and trangular. Its teeth wear away or fall out and new teeth from the row behind take its place

I like the Great white shark because it is strong and big

by Mark Weese
age 8

World of Nature

I like nature
because I like
the flowers
the sun the trees
the rabbits the birds

Our Wonderful World of Nature.

In this country we have lots of wildlife like rabbits, foxes, hedgehogs, deers and lots of other animals. They live in special homes in the forest all around the UK. In the winter animals hibernate. Hibernate means that they sleep in winter. These animals are interesting beacause they are good to watch.

By Shane Saunders age 8

Nature.

I Like Nature. Because I Like to go the seaside. Because. I can go in to caves. When I got in the caves. There I saw a Map. and then we Left.

Our Wonderful World of Nature

I have got two pets. One is a dog named Sadie and the other is a cat called Tash. Sadie has just turned one year old and Tash is twelve years old. Sadie is a golden retriever and my cat is black and white. My dog annoys the cat sometimes. I really like having pets. I have a pond in my garden and my dog drinks out of it in the summer when she is hot. My cat has eaten all the fish out of it so we have no fish left. I have one big tree in my garden that me and my sister climb up. We don't have any birds in our garden because my pet cat Tash chases them away.

by Leanne Warrender
age 9

I like my cats, because they are fluffy. And my cat lives in my home, AND I LIKE it. And I had got a dog, and a fish and a budcis and I like them all my pets

Danielle 6

Our Wonderful World of nature.

I have two dogs their names are Ben and Sam. I take them on walks in the woods. I have a parrot his name is Sam Bird. He bites alot but he does not hurt.

By Joanna Davies
age .8.

I like cats because you can play with them. I like to feed cats because they purr at you. In the night they come up to you.

Stephanie 7

Raptors

Birds of prey that hunt mainly by day are called raptors. They include egles veltures hawks and falcans. These are all members of the bird group falconiformes. A raptor's keen eyes can see victims thousands of metes away. I like birds very much.

by sean Burndred 9 years old

All the Animals of the Forest

Squirrels shoot through the trees like silver bullets.
A red flash through the green.
Collecting nuts for winter.
Foxes grey or red.
Low down looking for food all day long.
When there not hunting there sleeping!
Falcons, brown birds they are.
Winging their way through the trees.
Praying on small animals.
They sleep in the trees.

Owls smart old things they are.
White sometimes, oar brown.
They sleep in the day and hunt at night.
Why kill them?

By Adam Colclough

nature

My favourite animals are horses and rabbits. Because they are very loveing and I like fish to and Butterflys. I useto have some fish and two Rabbits and my Rabbits useto jump up and down on the grass

by Katie Burgess age 9

The tree

The tree stood firm
    and the wind blew hard.
The animals dance around the tree
    and God said let the
Eagle soar in the sky
    and the cheetahs run free.
The animal's
Said let us live in
Peace and
harmony

by Matthew Roberts

Our wonderful world of Nature

I think wildlife and sealife need to be looked after because if you cut down the trees in woods you will be cutting down animals homes. They will have no homes and if you cut down the trees in winter they will freeze to death and die. Sealife needs to be looked just a little bit more. If people go out in oil tankers sometimes they have a little too much oil in their tanks and it tips them. They let some oil out into the sea and it kills the fish and all the sealife. Animals are part of nature and my favourite animals are rabbits, hamsters, fish, horses, cats and dogs. My mum has lots of plants because she loves them. I like them too. I particularly like the ones that are colourful and smell nice. Which flowers do you like?

by Rachael Williamson
age 9

The new Forest.

The new forest is all nature.
There are daffodils, blue bells, leaves, beetles, ants,
wasps, bees and birds.
The fungus is growing on the trees
and all the oak trees are growing
and ivy going up the trees.
Tigers are roaming around the forest
and every thing to eat.

By Shaun Glover.

The Wonderful World of
    Nature

Nature is Cool
And you can be to
if you take care of it
The united Kingdom can be a better place
if you care

by Christopher Sproson Age 8

god made the beaytifnl synsnchefor us. Betnar

Nature

I like animals because I have a horse. His name is Joe I like horse riding and I go to Cauers Wall District horse show Joe is 6 years old and his Birthday is on april the 16th I Love Joe vrey much. He is good At Jourmping I put Joe in His Stable. And I go home to bed.

by Hayley Kalbell

Age 9

Dont cut elephonts' tusks off. Look after all animals.

Gary

nature

I like animals because I have got pets. I have got hamsters and a rabbit and a guinea pig. I also have cats and a dog some fish. In the summer my rabbit was not very well. So my mum put him on a lead and she let me take him out on the grass. His name is Benjamin Bunny. He **eats** carrots lettuce and dried rabbit food he drinks water.

By Emma
Louise Jennings.

Age 8.

Give animals somewhere nice to live. 🐶🐶🐶

Stacey

Nature

I like birds, Rabbits, cats and dogs. I have a friend who has lots of pet she is named Emma she as a rabbit called BenJamin Bunney. I have not seen BenJamin Bunney. Emma has a dog as well. I know Emmas dog alot

by Kate Littleton
AGe 9

Tigers and snakes live in the rain forest

Jayden

I like Ladybirds because I like The shiny black on Their red back. I like The other animals because I like Their skins. Because I like The colours on Their back. I like The flowers because I like The colours as well.

Amy 6

Elephants are safe in animal parks.

Christian

by
Alex Mitchell

Party down under

It was the 27th of February and it was Carl the kangaroo's birthday. Karen, his wife, told Winney and Wolly the wallabies to tell Carl's friends to come to my house, at 27 Kangys Close. It will be a surprise party. But don't tell Terry the Taipan because remember last time ..... "Yes", Winney said. So she went to tell his friends. Karen thought, "I will tell Carl go get the shopping then I will arrange the party." When Carl got in he heard Karen go into the garden, so he followed. "Surprise!" Then Carl said, "This is the best party ever!"

Dinosaurs lived a long long time ago.

Zoe.

Tiger and King Elephant

One day in the Zaire jungle king elephant was having a nap until he was woken by his messenger who said "your majesty! your majesty! the tigers are killing all the buffalos, the tiger leader says if you don't step down from the throne he's going to keep on killing." "Bring him in then!" "Now what's this about you wanting to be king?" "Oh yes I want to be king so I can kill diffrent animals like you." "No I will not step down." "Ok but I warned you." Then one day elephant was having a stroll when he trod on tiger who was asleep in the long grass. Then tiger was dead and elephant remained king of the Zaire jungle!

By Andrew Poole

Stephanie

The park is a beautiful place

Sleeping Animals

In a year the'ie are only four seasons.
Spring and summer are the best
time to see most animals.
Winter time is bad for them that
is why they sleep
That is when we come in we could
give them food to eat.
So maybe they could live another day
on their feet.

By Andrew Redfern

Animals of the Jungle

Every rabit, cat or dog once was wild and not a pet. But now the Jungles completeley ruined because poachers come with guns and nets to take them away to a cruel place to be locked up and sometimes never released and I think animals should run free and not be hunted for their fur

by matthew cartwright

Nature.

Nature is good. All these are wonderful things.
We cut down trees to make lots of Paper.
We are throwing animals homes away.
So please think twice about paper.

People tread on animals that is nature too.
We have pond's, flowers, trees and that is nature too
Animals should live day and night.
We should be thankful for the things we have.
Please help us to save things.

By Amy Thompson

look after our World

look after our World our beautiful World
For it is too nice to destroy.
our animals, our animals
are God's Creatures, all day and all night.
Don't pollute the air for it is a lovely breeze.
Don't chuck rubbish on the floor for it is too nice.
Never ever destroy the World because it is our home.

By

Kevin

Saunders

The Big Bonfire

When I went to the Rookery bonfire.
It was the biggest one. I ever had seen.
Plus I went with Wesley.
Wesley said what a bonfire.
Wesley started to run up to the bonfire. It was lit. He ran and ran and jumped and stopped a little boy from going in it.
I went to get something to eat.
I had chips fish and gravey with salt and vinegar.
Wesley had hot dog chips and onions.
It was great!

By Gregory Howell

Our wonderful world

Our wonderful world too good to lose.
All the beautiful creatures great and small.
Wildbeests, friendly creatures all too good
to lose. No matter what they are all to
good to lose. The world is so nice and so good.
The world would be nothing without
these lovely animals and trees.

by Gareth Lewis

Our Beautiful Nature.

Our nature's too beautiful to be killed.
It's so great we can not afford to lose it.
Oh, please, please don't cut down so many trees.
The're so many animals that we want to save.
Try not to pollute the air.
People building factories stop polluting streams.
Don't put litter on the floor.
Shooting foxes, birds & rabbits,
It's just got to stop.
Don't kill spiders the're nature too.
We need flowers, trees, crops, streams and most of all
We need animals to make Nature.

By Natasha Jones.

Our Wonderful World

Our world is definitely the best
If there was a competition
Earth would win the rest.
Flowers in the gardens all blooming colours
Reds, yellows, pinks, greens
Blues and oranges so it seems.
Trees so tall so healthy and green.
When Autumn comes there's blossom and buds that cover the trees.
Pollution kills our rivers and streams.
So keep everywhere nice and clean.

By Emma Rowell Dunne

Wild life

I LOVE wild life we couldn't do with out it. It is great there are so many other creatures too, like monkeys and lizards and other things too. So we should look after wild life. Yes we should and don't kill so many thing's for food. Please don't kill wild life

BY Wesley Holdcroft

Nature

You can not kill nature.
You can not burn the tree that the animals are living in.
We should not hurt the animals.
We should not kill animals for meat.
We should not kill animals.
We should not film the animals to show on the television

By Linda Lawton

Our wonderful world

Our wonderful is our world. but I must say we should care for our pets and our friends. I have got a very best friend. Her name is Emily Snape. She has got a dog and She cares for it. So our wonderful is our world.

By Samantha Smith

Nature

We really should look after trees and animals. Is we recycle paper.
It will save animals homes.
Nature's beautiful when we think.
With all the animals.
Some are big. Some are small.
Some fierce and some not. By Craig Humphreys

Nature's a wonderful thing.

Nature Nature bright and new. You had better look after it because it's for me and you.
In the skys I see birds. And in the garden blossoms emerge.
Up a tree a nest lies with chicks, twittering as the mother flies. A woodpecker pecking at a tree making a hole for his family.
As the squirrell collecting nuts hides them for the winter to come.

By Annabelle Werner.

My Nature poem

Nature is nice, nature is lovely.
Nature is sweet and sour.
All the animals running fast tripping over logs.
Deer and Antilope all quite the same.
Trees and flowers rising quick Just as lovely even with a snip.
It's not that wild, and not that slick, but flowers are growing lovely and quick.

By Mark Tagg.

Don't Throw Paper Away.

When you write and get it wrong then you throw that paper away and get some more. That's wrong too.
When you throw paper away do you know what you are really throwing away.
You are throwing away animal's homes so please please think twice about throwing paper away.

By Richard Poole.

THE ANIMAL PARK

One day I went toan animal park
to see the animals play .
But what a fabulous thing it was
on a warm summers day.

I saw a bear, honest I swear!
I saw a lion
its colour was rusty (like iron).
I saw a cat chasing a rat
my dad saw a monkey.
It was big fat and hunky.
my siser saw a frog as big as a dog!
I saw a deer drinking some beer.
I saw a giraffe having a laugh!
I saw some mice eating boiled rice.

My mum said she enjoyed the day
and now we must be on our way!

                              RachelMellor

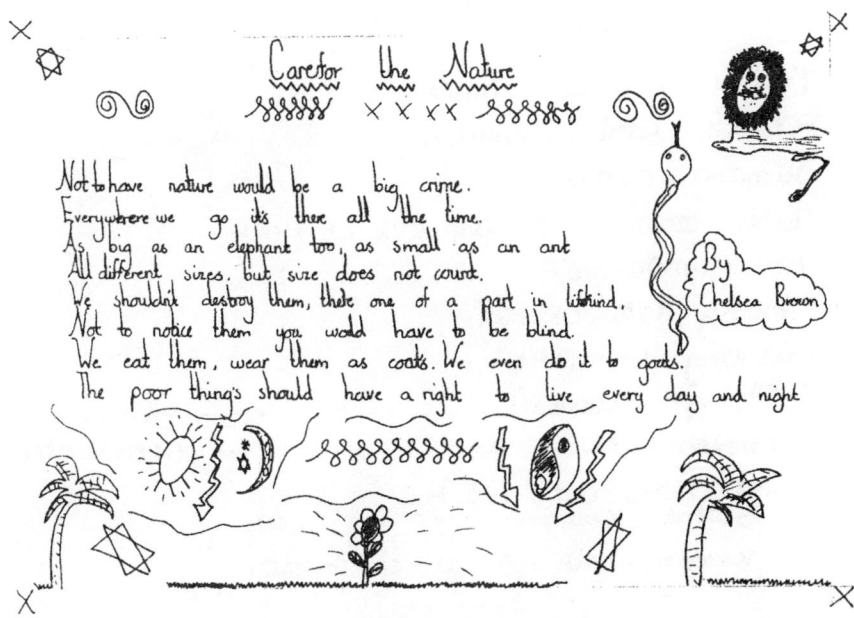

Care for the Nature

Not to have nature would be a big crime.
Everywhere we go, it's there all the time.
As big as an elephant too, as small as an ant
All different sizes, but size does not count.
We shouldn't destroy them, there one of a part in lifekind.
Not to notice them you wold have to be blind.
We eat them, wear them as coats. We even do it to goats.
The poor thing's should have a right to live every day and night

By Chelsea Brown

Gym Poem

Sport is my favourite thing
It makes me want to dance & sing
It makes me want to flick & summersalt
And do a very good handspring vault.

I want to do the best I can
and twirl around just like a fan.
You don't have to fear to be a gymnast
Just join and try hard and make it last.

by Michelle Oxley

Play

I like doing the splits and I like playing
hous because you have a dady.
And you can have kids

Emma c14

Sport.

Today I play games.
Football and tennis.
Jumping about.
Table tennis ball's pop out at you.
At gymnastics.
Having lots of fun.
Dancing to music.
All night long.
Running around the track.
My shoes are red hot
Sweat running off my head.
Keeping fit is what I do.

By Susan Greatbatch

Adam 6

I like natur. because of all the animals. my favourite animal is a beaver. I think beavers are very clever and very funny when they chop trees down. I think the lodge that they make is very good.

 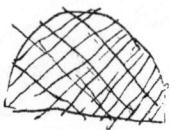

I like lions and tigers
I like them because they are colourful and furry

Simon 6

I like nature be cus it has animals and I like animels be cus I like cats and I like camels and I like horses and I like cows and I like cat and I like dogs and I like caberpielars be cus they eat and I like a animel.

chelse, is 6

nature I like
I like thm becase birds
fly.

Daniel. H.

Our wonderful world of birds of prey.
Birds of prey that hunt mainly by day are called raptors. They include Eagles, Vultures, Hawks and falcons. These are all members of the Falconiformes bird group. A raptors keen eyes can see victims thousands of metres away. Most can fly very fast, soar, dart and hover in one place. They have sharp curved beaks (bills) and talons (claws) to catch and rip up there prey.
   The Californian Condor is a spectacular bird, a great dark shape soaring on huge wings.
   When a King Vulture lands at a carcass in the jungle all the other birds leave.
   Vultures are natures recyclers. They clear up dead bodys, so nothing is wasted the turkey Vulture is very good at his job.
   The secretary bird prefers to walk rather than fly.
The Osprey is a superb fish-catcher. It flies high over the water, scanning the surface for fish and hovering occassionly for a better look
      by Craig Hughes Age 8

Ben P. 6

nature

I like nature because.
I like to go the seaside.
And I see caves.
And I see swim.
And I go swim.

I like animals because I like the colours on them. I like animals that live under water because they can swim. I like how they swim under water. It is good how they do it.

Laura >

World of Special People

I love hug him, My my rabbit Thumper because I
Mum loves him too.
Jessica Sherratt.
aged 5.

My brother John
is special to me

Alexandra Evans
aged 4.

My Dad is special he works with me.
Alexander Clarke aged 4.

I love my hamster
and I hold hold him
everyday.
Kerry-Ann Vaughan
aged 5.

my mum is speclal
she togords me
stories

Adam Brown
aged 4

Special people
my mum and Dad are special.
and people and God are Special.

Jodie Adams

my Nana is special
because she gives us
jigsaws.   By
claire   Hamnett
age 5

My Dad is spellal ne plays football with me.

Daniel Price. Aged 4.

I went to the zoo and I saw a horse.
Sarah Starkey aged 5.

My mum is special she meets me from school

Conor Sandiwell
aged 4

Police are special because they look after us and save us to.

by Abbey Smith
Age 5

My cat Thomas is special because he jumps on the window sill.

Ben Sandywell aged 4.

my special people
my Family and Friends we go Shopping we go for sweets at the shops and we go to parties.
by Matthew worthy

My Gran was special She always had lots of paper for us to colour on. By Ashley Hodgkinson Age 6

My Mum is special because she loves me.
Nathan Morrey aged 4.

My sister is special because she lets me play with her games.
by Stephanie Sims.
Age 6.

My brother is special to me he kisses me when I am upset.

By Zoey Watson age 5

Nana looked after me when I was poorly.

Rebecca Goodwin aged 4.

My mum is special because she loves me alot.

Natalie Hunt aged 5.

My Grandma is special because she gives me sweets.

Age 6

Laura Daniels

My Grandad is special because he takes me for walks. By Katie Gough Age 6

The policeman looks After our houes

By Laura Dixon age 5

By Shaun Slater Age 5
The Lolly Pop Lady helps me cross the road

My Grandad is special because he takes me for walks

by Cheryl

Age 6

My mum is special because she looks after me.

By Daniel
Age 5

I love you

Animals are special because we have to look after them

aged 4

Jackie Sallis

RYA Jam

The Lolly Pop Lady helps us cross the road. She is special

Age 5

My friends are special because We Can have a Party

by
Thomas Challinor
Age 6

Elephants are special they live in the jungle.

Katrina Johnson
aged 4.

Katrina

Policemen are special people because they look after us.

By Carl Lear Age 6

Albert's car. Aged 4.

Zoe West Age 5

My dad is special because he brings me presents.

Elephants are special.

Kyle Taylor aged 4

An elephant.   Jackie Sallis aged 4.

By Nicola Age 5

My Grandad is special because he gives me chocolate.

My mummy is special because she is kind to me.
By Melissa Poole
Age 5

I love my teacher because she teaches her children.

By Kirsty
Age 6.

World of Wishes

I wish my Dad would take me to a football match

Age six 6
By
Liam Highfield

I wish I was a king. I would live in a palace and I could have all the gold in the world. I would be rich and I would give to the poor so they can be anything they want.

by Dean Towers

I wish I could fly to the Isle of White for a holiday
By Jodie Frost
Age 6.

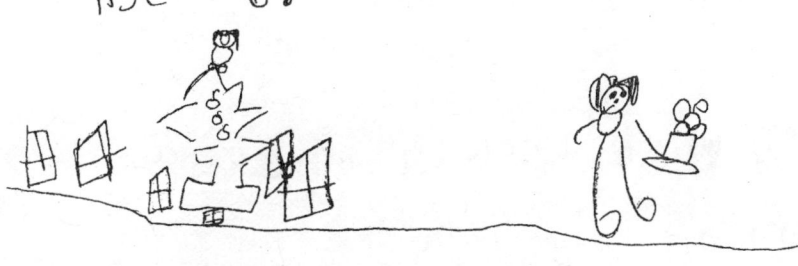

I Wish I had a racing car with a seatbeltandaPhone by Jessica Bossons

I wish it was summer I could go in the swimming pool

by Donna Thompson

I wish I could ride on a train. By Alex Smith. age 6.

I wish I had some money to spend I would have lots of yummy cakes.

by Jamie Cook.

I wish I could go to the Fair
By Jade Goodwin
Age 6

I wish I was rich so that I could go on a holiday to Turkey. BY LISA DAVIS Age 6

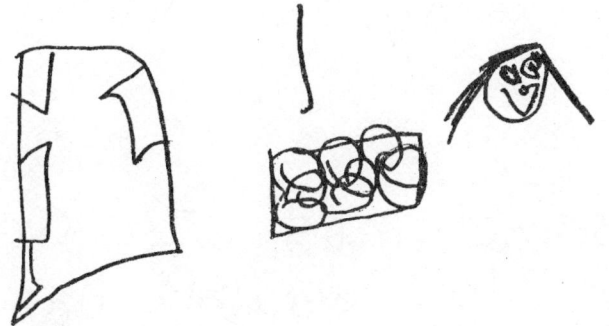

I wish for a dog and cat. KAREN LITTLETON

wishes   Kirsty oweng

I wish I could have a unicorn I would call it Victoria. I would fly to Spain. I would live there I would get a hotel. I would go on holiday to Greece. I would have some fish and chips and fly back to Spain

Sometimes I wish that we didn't have to go to school.

By Rebecca Warrender
Age 5

Sometimes I wish my dog would dance with me
By Victoria Foster
Age 6

my wish

my wish is for a motorbike

because you have fun.

But you will hurt yourself

Philip Grocott

I wish my rabbit would dance with me
By Lauren

Age 5

My wish that I coud fly

I woud fly to Affica I could see the

Liars and zebra So I could Play

with Tem

Ashley Michalak

I wish I had a tarantula because I like spiders.

By Joshua Lawton.

I wish I was eight because it would be my birthday by sarah snape

Sometimes I wish that my sister could come to school with me

by

Age 5 Koltie Wain

I wish I could be Queen

By Alexandra Eardley

Age 5

I wish it was my Birthday every day
By Nicole Eardley
Age 5

Sometimes I wish it was Christmas every day so that I could have lots of Presents.
By Sean Smithson
Age 5

Sometimes I wish that I could be a real live Barbie.
Age 6 Karina Boote

Sometimes I wish I could go to the zoo
BY Elizabeth.
Age 5

I wish I could fly and then I would not have to climb trees.
by Mark Young
Age 6.

I wish that I had a horse with wings.

by Charlotte
Age 5

...I wish that I was a fireman

By matthew Shipley Age 5.

I think my baby will be special. I'm going to take care of it.
by Damian.
Age 6.

I wish I could ride on my bike.

By Christopher Roberts.

I wish for an easter egg because I love chocolate.

by catherine phillips

I wish I was Jean Luc Picard on the Starship Enterprise.
John Jackson. Aged 4 years.

I would wish for a long dress and I would wear it all the time It would be pink with pink flowers and pink high-heeled shoes

Zoe Roberts

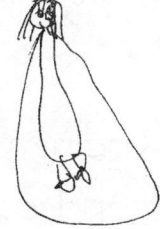

I wish I could be a fairy and I would fly to London and look for Santa.

Naomi Fox aged 4.

My Wish.
I wish sara lion and I would play with it.
Ian Howle

I wish for a mouse as a pet because I like mice.

by kyle chesters

I wish that my Barbie was alive then I could show my mum my friend.

By Katherine Leonard.

Wishes

I wishe for a Lion I will feed HiM in tha garden.

Lee frost

Wishes

I wish I was a bird because I could fly away and I wish that I was a rich man so I could buy a crown, then I would be the king. Then I would be rich for good

I wish that I was a cat because I could go on the roof and eat cat food but I would not die. I want to be a cat.

Timothy Callaghan

My wish

I wish that I had a sega because I have always wanted a sega. and I would play on it all the time with loads of games to it. I would have ten games or twenty games.

by Stellina Jennings.

My Wishes

I wish that I would come to school every day cause I love school I love writing

Wonderful things I have done
I love Maths it is The ~~best~~
thing I ever do.

Gary Potts

I wish I was at Disneyland with Mickey and Minnie mouse

Lucy

My World of Wishes

If I had 100 wishes first I would wish for a game boy and second I would wish for some clothes but third my mum said wish for a horse I said yes but I wouldnt know what to wish for next. by Stephanie Longshaw.

I wished I was in a new house Now I am. I like it.

Mathew

I wish I was a shop keeeeeper in a baking shop.

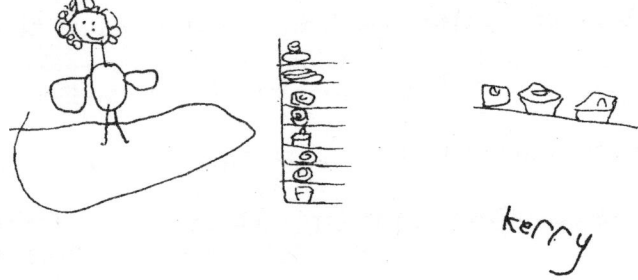

kerry

My wonderful wishes xxxxx
I wish for a big mansion because they are very nice. I would clean it every day. I would buy a car to go on holiday. When I come home I would relax and khaks it folks. by samantha gibson. xxx

I would want a hamster and I'd play with him

by Ashley Jones

I wish I had a blue.

Danielle Starkey

I wish Mrs Hughes could be my mum because I like her.

by Benjamin Lewis

The Farm My Hobby

I get up at 7.0.0 on every morning and I feed my cows and leed my Geese out then I get dressed for school. I have a good (bu) day at (shcol) school I get (I get) home I feed my cow agan and I get (s) on my truck to get some silage to feed the cows and the horses I get some straw and then when I have done my work I have my tea.

by

James age 9

Hobbies

Hello my name is Hannah I live with my mum Dad and brother. My favourite hobby is horse riding but I dont go very often so I ride my bike. I have lots of pen friends so I write a lot. I like playing in the snow. I don't like to tidy up because it is very boring.

Hannah Coclough
age 7½

I wish my mum won the Lottery. Then we will go to Disneyland. I wish my dad would buy me a hamster I will look after it

By Andrea Dzik

age. 8

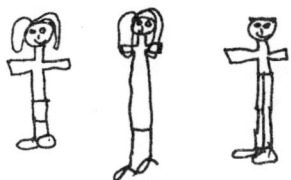

I wish my house could turn into a jungle and I could sleep outside.
DANIEL Jones. aged 5.

I wish

I wish that all the poachers would
stop spoiling the homes for the
wildlife. And start to help the wildlife
and plant some more trees.

The End

age 8½

By Koslie Vaughan

LUCY Hasey. 5.

IF I had a wish

If I had a wish. I would wish for my nan to come back alive because I've never seen her. She died twelve years ago three year before I was born so she never saw me but she saw my cousin Leigh and she didn't see my other cousin Kylie.

by Thomas Thorley
age 9

It I was an elephant I would squirt water over all the children.

Jodie

I love to play in the waves at the seaside

Lyren

Once I wished I was strong I wished it came true then I wished down the wishing well but it did not come true. Then I went around the back yard. I found a wishing star I wished I had a rabbit it came true.

by Katie halliwen age 7

One day I wish that I could have some chocolate and pizzas and chip then I went to the park then I went to my friends then we went to the river we got some wahtr from the river.

By Richie Cahill
age 9

I would like to be an astronaut. I would go to the moon.

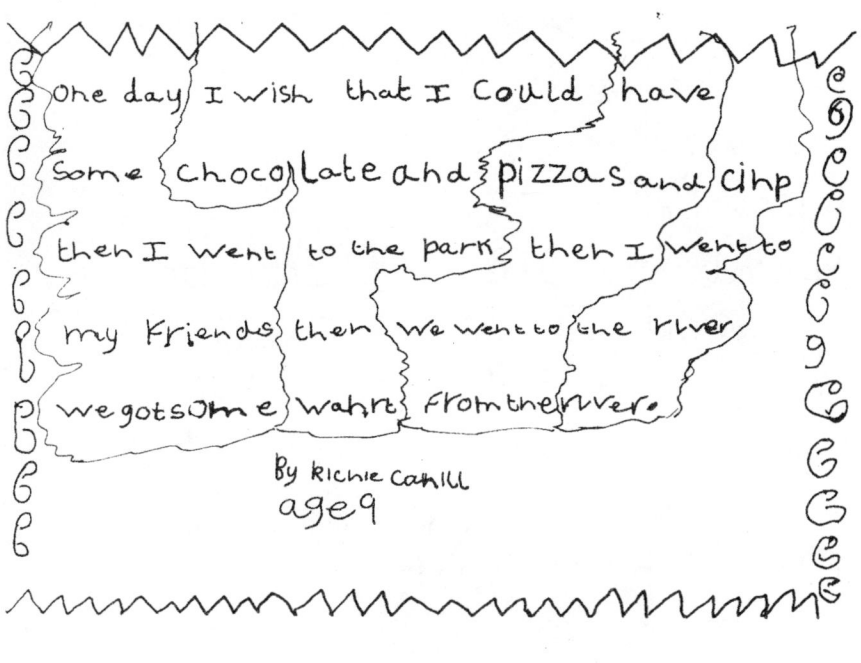

Simon

Wishes by Greatbatch Steven

If I had a wish I would wishes for a bike. I would ride around the block on it. I would have races on it. I would go for bike rides down the fields. I would wish for a silver bike with gears.

I wish I could go on the Ark with all the animals

Addison

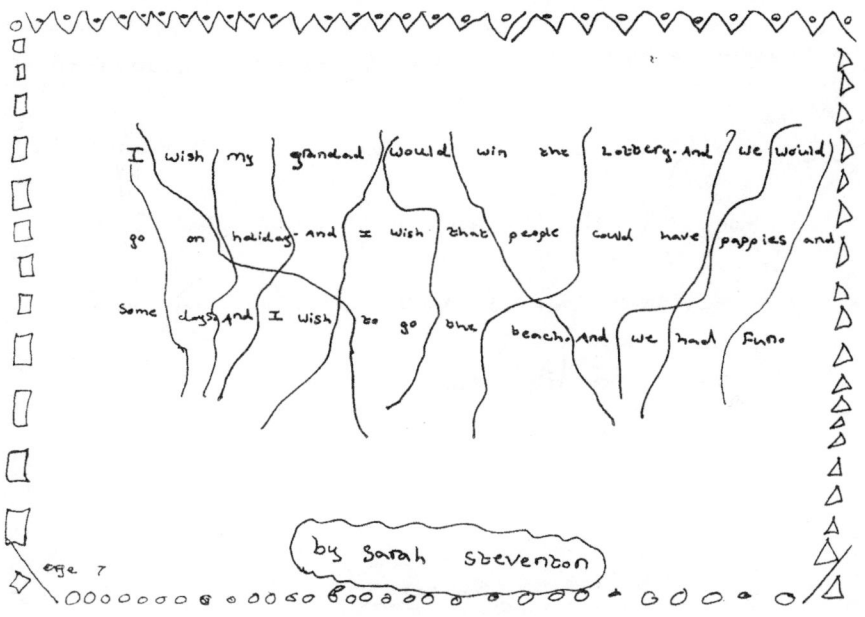

I wish my grandad would win the Lottery. And we would go on holiday. And I wish that people could have puppies and some dogs, and I wish to go the beach. And we had fun.

by Sarah Steventon

age 7

I wish for some money for the poor They can Buy food and drinks of orange Juice and some clothes that they can wear

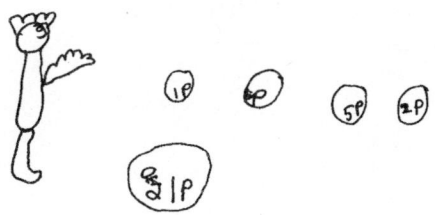

age 8

BY Jeanne

I wish These would have Money who haven't got money. I wish I went on holiday sow I can go to the beach and I will go in the sea and I will swim in the sea.

by Rebecca Burgess Age 7

I Wish I had a horse to ride on it and to jump over fences and it had wings to fly to The land of Nowhere.

Age 9   by Ben eyles

The 2 wishes.

Katie was woken by the telephone ringing. She jumped up and hurriedly got dressed. She went downstairs and ate her breakfast. She was going out today with her best friend Emma. They were going to the woods. Emma called for her at 11o'clock. They ran down to the woods and began to climb some trees. Emma fell out of a tree and fell on a stone. She saw the stone sparkle but she just took no notice of it because she thought she was imagining things. "Hey have you seen that new bike on television? I wish I had that" BANG!!! "WOW," said Emma. "It's that bike on television, this stone must be a wishing stone" said Katie. "Come on let's wish for another bike for me" said Katie. "O.K." "I wish for another bike for Katie" said Emma. "Wow" "Come on lets leave some more wishes for another time for when we really need them." said Katie. "Come on lets go and tell our parents." said Emma." And the two of them skipped off into the sunshine.

By Jayne Simm.

---

age 7 JON

I would wish for a horse that could fly. I would fly to America and have some chicken and chips.

Jonathan Grocott.

Wishes By Rebecca Holmes

I wish for a unicorn a magic unicorn. It will fly me where ever I wanted. It will be a white unicorn. When I want it to do something I would put magic dust on it. It will have silk fluffy fur. It will have a golden collar. It will say her name on it her name will be sagar

 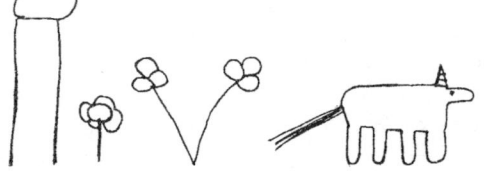

wishing wishing well
I'll drop a penny
down your well
and turn you in to
a wizard well.

Dean Williamson Class 6

I wish I could have a horse as a special treat.

Lucy-Hosey
aged 5.

I wish I had a horse to ride on and I would clean his stable.

by Hannah Bloor

World of Fantasy

Matthew & Daniel   matthew Gillan   age 8

One day there where two boys. They were very small. They fell down a hole. There was a big mole robot. I trod on a hammer. Me and Daniel smashed the mole Daniel said there is a key. Daniel said I see a door. I said use the key the key want in I turned the key the key turned and the door opened we went in the room and I trod on a whip. I saw a lion I whipped the lion it died. There was a teleporter it teleported us back home.

In our classroom there are six children. and some children have got glasses and there is a green boy and his name is john and he is six years old and he is in class 6m he has got green hair and green spots.

by kimberley moseley

age 9

Trouble in the forest

Biscuit was a squirrel who lived in a magical animal world. He lived with all his friends, but there's something Biscuit didn't like. He's one of the smallest animals in the forest. There was a wolf in the forest, a real baddy. His name was Ben.

Louise was a horse, a magical horse and she loved Joal. Joal was a male horse and he was very handsome and was loved by all the female horses and even other animals.

One day Ben, the wolf, threatened to burn down the forest because he was jealous of all the animals. So Joal went to talk to him. When Joal came back he was badly hurt because Ben had bitten him hard.

So Oddy the owl made him better by sprinkling some magic powder on Joal's leg and then Oddy put a bandage on it so the pwder wouldn't fall off.
It only took 3 days for Joal's leg to heal.

Ben wanted to hurt Joal again so he thought up a plan to capture Louseal.....

Jessica Barnes

Snow Ball

My little friend.
Whistling through space.
Up to a planet that is so small.
It is called pubo.
It is very cold.
And my snowball misses it.

By Kacey Smith

age 8

Fantasy

One day in the middle of the summer Johno and Mathew wanted a lion but thir mum and dad would not let them have one. So after they had tea Johno and Mathew went to the park and they went to sit down under a tree. It had a door so they had a look.

They opened the door. A big draught pulled them in. There was a fairy. She said "You can have one wish or maybe two if you're good boys." Johno and mathew wanted a lion. "Our first wish will be a lion." "what will your next wish be?" "will you get us out of this place" "o.k but one more thing", I cannot get you a lion for life! but you can adopt one" o.k. "Here you are how many tickets do you want?" "We only want one because we are going to share it we'd better be going now bye.

They went round and round and round and round and they landed on the bed and jumped under the sheets. Night mum I must be imagining things mum said.
BY
KERRIE WATSON

One day millions of years ago there was a god who took a sun and put it into the sky but one day the suns got bored of being on there own so they decided to go out and play so they did but it got to hot so yi came along and killed the nine suns and yi left one sun left.

by Richard M
Age 10

The princess and the dream

It was a sunny day and the princess was happy.
Her mum was going to give her a crown to wear at her next party.
The princess whose name was Jasmine was going to the Royal Palace.
She looked wearing beautiful dress.
During the party the King said "hello my dear, are you all right?" "yes"said
the princess.
   The Queen gave her the crown from a box and placed it on the princess's
head. Jasmine was so very happy that she said "thank you very much."
   The prince said "hello" to Jasmine and they danced all night,they got
married and lived happily ever after.
   A loud knock on the door woke Jasmine from her sleep, and she realised it
was all a dream!

               By
                 Kathryn
                    Burgess

The ghost who Lives in My house.

One day I sitting in My house.
one My seat in My Living Room
I switched on the T.V. and I was
Just geting cumfty when some thing
Moved of the shelf and it Broke. no
one was. I was in the house on
My own. It was spooky. By LISA PAlin
   Age 11

The Amazing Forest

When you go in to the magic forest
You'll surely be amazed.
The sun is a honey gold,
The clouds are sugar icing,
You can eat anything (I'm told).
The trunks of trees are chocolate.
The leaves are made of mint,
Daffodils are sugar diamonds.
Find the flower
From your dream.
Anything you think of will come   true.

                                            by Nicholas Ellerton.

wishy washy

Wishy washy was a magice cat, ifact he was a withes cat. He was miss cacats cat. She was no ordinary catch who had a wond & a book of spells she had magic blomers! they were red & wite with the occasional bat and spider.

one day as she was reading the 'Daily Bore' she saw an advert for a singing contest is the villig hall. The only problem was she had a horebel shrill voice. She put on the blomers & gave her self an operatic voice. Poor old wishy didn't like her singing at the best of times but when she had an operatic voice he had to do some thig.

It was the day of the contest & she was half way thew her aria when wishy jumpd up on stage and ripd of her blomers. Well you should of seen the andience they wher tumbeling with laghwer at her horebel voice & not to mection bear bottom! that night when she was liying down (because of the inkars nest? wishy whent out to the all night cleners & you will never guess what he did he washd them! They were all white & bruner she had to fly them back to reatc it. Didn't tacke long for the bats & spiders to start clinging but oh wate a site it was

So if you see a witch on a broon strik withth a cat with a hat & a wich with small blomers you know its miss cacet & wishy!

by
Samantha
Sims
age 11

I like having dreams because
I have nice dreams. I dream
about my mummy and I dream
about nice things

Stacy 6

Green Hill Zone

Emma and Victoria lived with their mum and sister. They both loved to play on their computer. But one peculiar day they were playing and something strange happened.

It was about 3:55pm after school Monday afternoon. The girls were playing. Suddenly they were zapped through the screen!! They were in the Green Hill Zone with Sonic, Tails, and Doctor Robotnic. "We must defeat him!" said Sonic. Suddenly their bodies were not their own. Their little sister Julie was messing with the controls! They were jumping, turning all over the place. Then there was a big FLASH !

They fought as hard as they could. It looked as though Robotnic was going to beat them. Then they won him and came out of the screen..... Three weeks later they sold the Mega Drive.

Gemma Warrender

The Ghost By Daniel Johnson

One day I went into a ghost house.

I saw a ghost I ran up the statas.

He flooed out of now here it was night I was scared.

I could not get out I had to sleep there.
The ghose had a parge the next morning I got out.
and went home

age 8

Daniel & Matthew

Danny. Smith

one day there were two boy's they are very small and thay lived in a vinger bottle. There names are matthew & Daniel one day matthew & Daniel went for a walk and as they went by they saw george the rabbey and he said hallow and they lived happeyle ever after. By Danny lee smith 6m

age-9

My ghost storie

One day a ghost came and found another Ghost and the ghosts found a door. And then the ghosts has not been seen again.

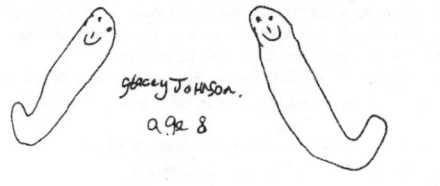

Stacey Johnson.
age 8

REAMON THE SELFISH DRAGON

In a land far away where no dreams can take you there lived a very selfish dragon. His name was Reamon. He was so selfish that he never gave any of his powers away to the other dragons and never shared his jewels or rubies. Then one day he sat on a chair and it broke.

So he went to see if Fixit dragon would fix it. He said "NO I WON'T! FIX IT YOURSELF! You don't share any of your gifts so I don't see why I should." Reamon went home and cried then one of his tears fell on a chair leg and it stuck together.

Reamon said to himself I don't need any of them other dragons. Then he realised that his hands were stuck together. He was shouting out but no one heard him and there he died of starvation the very next day.

BY
LAUREN
GALLIMORE

the trap door

One day there was a trap door waiting to be opened for the things waiting to cume out sow if you see it then you wud be its slave forever. the End

By Lloyd Littleford

THE PLANT THAT SPOKE

Today was the most unusual day of my life, as if it isn't bad enough already. I have a brother who thinks he's the next David Attenborough, he's even changed his name to David, mad or what!! I have a sister who thinks the song could you be the most beautiful girl in the world was wrote for her, my dad wears a wig and I think my mum and I are the only sane ones in the family. Today started off as normal as can be expected we went shopping, BORING!!!!!!
My mum bought a funny looking plant.
Later on in the sitting room I heard a strange voice it said "my name is Polly what is yours?" It spoke in a squeaky kind of voice. I said "are you speaking to me?"
The voice spoke again "well I don't see anyone else around here do you?"
This time I looked round, there stood on the window sill, the funny looking plant mum had brought, singing Saturday night and doing the dance. "Saturday night dancing I like the way you move pretty baby." I went and told my mum, but she didn't believe me.
That night there was a huge BANG, the plant had fallen over the saucepan in the kitchen while dancing. Everyone went downstairs to see what all the noise was about, they saw the plant singing and dancing.
My mum thinks it's a pain when it doesn't shut up singing. I think it's dead funny.
My sister said it's giving her spots. My dad's taken his wig off in shock
and my brother, well he thinks it's amazing (with a capital A)

By Amy Louise Pawezowski.

Over the rainbow

Long ago Zoe and Maria went for a walk. They saw a rainbow. At the begining of the rainbow there were footprints a cm long. They started to follow the footprints. At the middle of the rainbow they met up with a goblin. The goblin's name was toothpick. "At the end of the rainbow there is a pot of gold" said toothpick. "If you help me find it I will give you half" he said. "O.K" said Zoe and Maria together. When they got the gold he kept it all to him self. Zoe and Maria went to the elves. They ran upto an elf. "Toothpick the goblin has all the gold" said Zoe. "We will blow the castle down and get the gold back" said Saukky. "Can we help" said Maria. They all went to the castle. They blew it up and the gold flew everywhere! Zoe and Maria had tea with the elves then followed the rainbow home and never told anyone about it.

By Sarah moseley

THE BEGINNING oF THE FROG

Once upon a time there lived a demon. He lived in the centre of the earth . He had one eye of fire. he didin't have a right eye. He said one of these days I am going to make an animal. I will call it a frog.

one day he crushed a rock and made it in to a powder. After about 4 thousend years hemade some clay After about another 3 thousend years it was in shape. He put the colour into him one day he started to cry the teers dripped on the frog and gave him a heart and all he needed.

He had'nt been out for 7 thousend years. He went out and told god will you blow life into him.god said '' ok '' and got it out of his hand. He blew life into him god gave the demon the frog back he played and played with him under the ground. the frog got bored and hopped out to the wild the demon woke up and said oh no hes ran away he got up he got up and went out and ''said come back you rotten thing''he went out searching but never found him.

by

philip Reynolds

The girl who sits next to me

The girl who sits next to me
Has alot to say
Her eyes are very creepy
She always stares at me
She asks me questions
that do not make sense.
She talks all day long
She laughs like a horse
She eats very little.
But she loves gymnastics.
She sings all day long
When shes in a mood
She does her work

By Sarah Mitchell

World of Celebrations

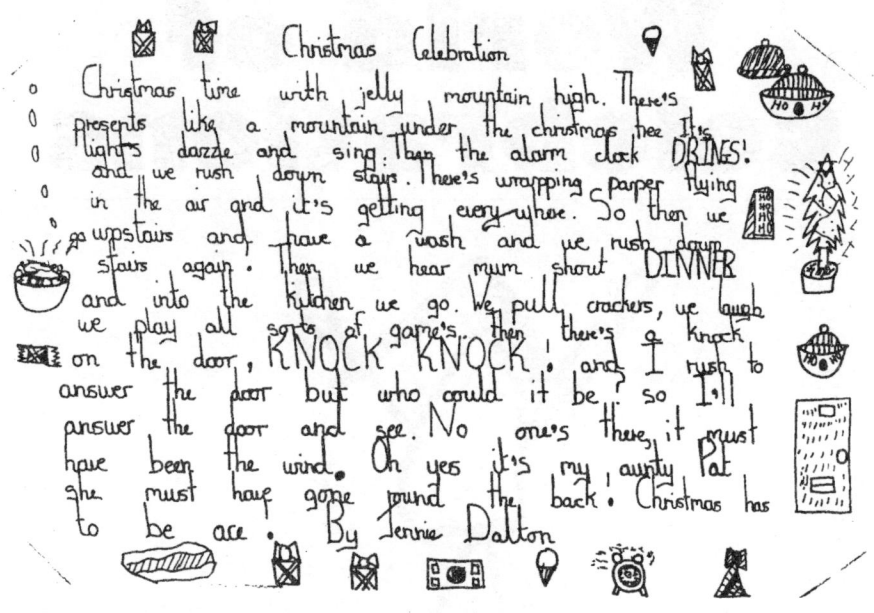

Christmas Celebration

Christmas time with jelly mountain high. There's presents like a mountain under the christmas tree. It's lights dazzle and sing. Then the alarm clock DRINGS! and we rush down stairs. There's wrapping paper flying in the air and it's getting everywhere. So then we go upstairs and have a wash and we rush down stairs again. Then we hear mum shout DINNER and into the kitchen we go. We pull crackers, we laugh we play all sorts of game's. Then there's a knock on the door, KNOCK KNOCK! and I rush to answer the door but who could it be? So I'll answer the door and see. No one's there, it must have been the wind. Oh yes it's my aunty Pat she must have gone round the back! Christmas has to be ace. By Jennie Dalton

The Celebration

When it is your birthday you have a great big party.
When it is your birthday you have a birthday cake.
When it is your birthday you have a lot of presents.
When it is your birthday you play lots of games.
When it is your birthday people come to visit.
When it is your birthday you play pass the parcel.
When it is your birthday you have alot of fun.

by Rachael Tarrant

Christmas

Christmas! It's a time for happiness
'Rip' 'Rip' Oh it's a superlooper waterpistol.
Thanks mum. Thanks dad.
'Rattle' 'Rip' Oh it's a water game
Thanks 'Santa'.
'Woof' 'Woof' What's that noise? It's a 'Puppy'.
Christmas is the best day ever for 'Children'.

By Mark Gould.

Kay's birthday

On Monday Kay got up she was excited because
It was her birthday,
She went down stairs for breakfast,
There were loads of presents waiting,
She shouted, "Mum I am opening my presents mum";
She opened one, "Yey its a dolly,"
She opened the second, "Its a game called the game of life."
"Oh what a nice!...a nice birthday I am having"

By Natalie Caton

Celebrating Time's

Celebration time has gone
And all our present's too
All the things we loved at christmas
Have all come and gone
But we'll only know that christmas is once a year
Christmas will come around again
And all our present's too
By
Gary Golden

Celebrations All Around

There are celebrations all around.
Christmas trees on the ground.
Lots of presents at Christmas time.
Easter is special too.
At Easter time there's chocolate eggs.
Yum! Yum!
Christmas Santa will come.
But that's not the real celebration.
At Christmas Jesus was born.
by Emily Snape